# Hmm!

Simple thoughts and reflections

Anne Eidschun

Hmm! Simple thoughts and reflections

Copyright © 2006 by Anne Eidschun

All Rights Reserved. No part of this work covered by the copyrights hereon may be reproduced or copied in any form or by any means - graphic, electronic, or mechanical, including photocopying, recording, taping, or information storage and retrieval systems - without written permission of the author.

Published by Aztec Book Publishing
1606 Delaware Avenue
Wilmington, DE 19806

ISBN-13: 978-0-9787674-3-3
ISBN-10: 0-9787674-3-8

Printed in the United States of America
at Aztec Copies, Inc. in Wilmington, Delaware

Cover Design: J. McVeigh

This book may be ordered directly from the author.
Your comments and thoughts are always welcome.
Email address: Hmmsimplethoughts@comcast.net

## Dedication

I would like to humbly dedicate this collection

To...

Bill.
The man in my life
who gives me inner peace.

My family - especially
my brother, Bob, and my sister, Barbara -
no matter what I do they all think it's great!

Amee and Stacy - my miracle children
who always encourage me
and include me in their lives.

My friends - who always treat me
like family.

And

Lassie -

Over all her years,
she listened to all my thoughts and reflections
and always gave me an approving grin.

## About the Author

For the past 25 years I have occasionally taken pen to paper. It never was my intention to expose my writing to knowing smiles. I suppose I might have been concerned that my English teacher, Mrs. Finnigan, wherever on earth she is now, would have a fit with my flair for poetic license!

Now that I am over 50, I am learning that you can take license with many more things than just poetry and that suits me fine.

This collection could be one of many if you read it and tell your friends and relatives to try and buy a copy at the nearest bookstore. If you decide to sip a glass of wine or chug a beer and leisurely read and enjoy my thoughts and reflections – never to share with anyone but yourself – that is okay, too. As a very dear 95 year old man named Ed once said to me...."whatever floats your boat!"

Anne

# Thoughts and Reflections

Birds ..................................................................... 2
Palmetto Dunes ................................................... 4
War ....................................................................... 6
Perfect Vacation ................................................. 8
Commitment ..................................................... 10
One of a Kind .................................................... 12
Happy Birthday! ................................................ 14
The Sea .............................................................. 16
So much...So little ............................................ 18
Black ................................................................... 20
First ..................................................................... 22
The Secret ......................................................... 24
Surprise .............................................................. 26
Perspective ....................................................... 28
Living ................................................................... 30
It Was Blue ........................................................ 32
Extra Steps ........................................................ 34
Children's View ................................................. 36
On Vacation ....................................................... 38
Fifty Years .......................................................... 40
I Feel Like A Child ............................................ 42
Friend .................................................................. 44
Hope .................................................................... 46
Decisions ............................................................ 48
The Day .............................................................. 50

v

| | |
|---|---|
| It Is So Hard | 52 |
| Remember | 54 |
| Mending | 56 |
| What Does it Mean? | 58 |
| Lassie | 60 |
| Children | 62 |
| Mellow | 64 |
| From Nowhere | 66 |
| Clouds | 68 |
| Footprints | 70 |
| Rhythm | 72 |
| She | 74 |
| Gifts | 76 |
| Explore | 78 |
| Perfect | 80 |
| On A Winter Night | 82 |
| It's Never Enough | 84 |
| And So | 86 |
| Once | 88 |
| The Third Dimension | 90 |
| Notre Dame | 92 |
| The Kiss | 94 |
| The Greatest Gift | 96 |
| EPILOGUE…JUST FOR YOU | 98 |
| IMAGINE | 100 |

Hmm...

!

Hmm...

# Birds

Swarming.

White.

So many over head.

All at once
over just one person.

A kite in the distance
surviving the wind.

The flyer is strong.

Everyone is watching.

That is...
the few that can take the cold.

Are the birds watching everyone
or
are they angels
just protecting one?

Hmm...

## Palmetto Dunes

An odd name
but a famous place.

I only think of a huge
uninvited guest.

When I did visit,
I touched and
only noticed
a beautiful flower.

No one around to give
me the name.

I walked on and looked back.

What a beautiful flower.

Hmm...

## War

*A raw truth.*

*What a shame.*

*Sad.*

*Hurtful to all – some
more than others.*

*Language is not enough
to explain or solve it.*

*It just is.*

*For now.*

Hmm...

## Perfect Vacation

2 people.

1 dog if desired.

Sports equipment.

Nice location.

Comfortable car.

Money to use wisely.

Water to look at or drink.

Clothes on your back.

Detergent!

Hmm...

## Commitment

You have the ring
because I love you
and you wanted a commitment-
of sorts.

My heart is different
in a small but important way.

Commitment for me
has to be on my terms.

I said I didn't know
if or when,
but know that I love you.

When my love is unconditional,
I will remove your ring and
place it on your hand again.

Forever.

Hmm...

## One of a Kind

A $1 would have no meaning.

A Strawbridge shirt
is made for someone else.

You took the time
and found
a shell.

One of a kind.

You gave it to me.

It's priceless.

One of a kind.

Like you.

Hmm...

## Happy Birthday!

If it's not your birthday,
I will call you for the next 364 days.

Eventually,
I will get it right!

Hmm...

## The Sea

What is it about the water?

Is it the majesty?

The other sounds
that are nearby?

It actually scares me,
but also soothes.

How is that possible?

Hmm...

Hmm...

## So much...So little

Listen to the birds.

Why is their squeaking
and chirping
more peaceful as we age?

The finest restaurant.

The best food.

Can't hear the people
at the table.

Everything becomes annoying
when not perfect.

Enjoying a peaceful dinner
takes effort.

The birds.

How do they accomplish
so much with so little?

Hmm...

# Black

Can be a despairing color
or one of elegance.

There's a room.

A black piano.

Singer with a simple strapless,
black dress.

Singing.

No one is there.

The room is empty.

Except for a feeling.

The singer stops.

Almost as in mid air
and glances in a mirror.

No one is there.

The man in a tuxedo
walks away.

Then turns
and extends his hand.

I must go.

Hmm...

## First

A great idea
or so I thought.

Already had it
manufactured and sold.

I thought it would sell
for $1.99.

Oh no...

I found it being sold
for 99 cents.

Bought 4!

Is this one more example
of mental telepathy?

Next time I have to be first!

Hmm...

## The Secret

Corporate life
begins as a great security.

Comfort.

Assurance.

Importance.

Self esteem.

Success.

As we reevaluate,
it is for many...

Stressful.

Demeaning .

Shortens life.

Time to begin again.

Hmm...

# Surprise

Anticipate a wonderful
relaxing time in an indoor Jacuzzi
filled with shampoo!

An unconventional way to
create bubbles.

The water just about
covers the jets
and you must turn them off!

Wine ready, pillow...
Muscles anticipating.

Oh, dear.

Mountains of bubbles.

Magazine wet, wine not as enticing.

All is not lost.

Used to the sound of jets.

Never really listened to the sound of bubbles.

A quiet crackling
like small popcorn kernels
reaching an edible state.

What started as anticipation
became a disappointment.

And then delightfully...the sound of bubbles!

Hmm...

## Perspective

An instant camera.

A novice photographer.

Two choices.

Horizontal or vertical
approach to the subject.

Today for no reason
I stood amongst the trees
and looked up.

Camera poised.

Click and
click again.

Looking upwards towards
the trees.

The sky has embraced the trees.

Can't wait to see the photograph.

Or is it better in my mind?

Hmm...

# Living

*Work.*

*Work.*

*Life style.*

*Family.*

*Things.*

*Happiness.*

*And now...*
*Age 50.*

*Is it a welcomed milestone?*

*Everything changes.*

*Flexibility.*

*Intuition.*

*Joy.*

*Seeing things never seen.*

*Living within means.*

*No medication.*

*Living every day.*

*Uncompromised.*

Hmm...

# It Was Blue

Found a new truck today.

Been working on it for months.

Don't like the salesperson.

The process has been painful.

I just need a truck
for the special things
I do.

Some are work.

Some are pleasure.

If we were all dogs,
we would know how to keep it simple.

Just take the truck you want
and pay me later.

Hmm...

## Extra Steps

*Not everyone hears it
or understands it.*

*Even after lessons.*

*Some think it is work related.*

*Wins the "quality" award
or a fancy certificate.*

*Might be a baby step
after the first.*

*If you dream…*

*Sway.*

*Listen.*

*Touch.*

*It's the extra beat.*

*Dancing.*

Hmm...

Hilton Head Island, South Carolina
2003

# Children's View

Walking the beach early morning,
March 27, 2003.

Parents with their children.

Every few steps another fort
protected by surrounding
walls, tunnels, bridges -
All using sand, shells and dry bamboo.

A psychiatrist's haven…
Perhaps a parent's nightmare.

A child's way of letting us know
they count on us to protect them.

The children stand proud, triumphant.

Looking to the adults.

Assuring them.

It is okay.

Some day we will be at peace, Mom and Dad.

Hmm...

## On Vacation

*It is sunny and warm
down South.*

*If you are in the North,
have a cup of tea.*

*I understand it warms the soul.*

Hmm...

## Fifty Years

Fifty years gone by.

Long ago friends.

Some have more.

Some think they have less.

But nothing has really changed.

Smiles are broader.

Laughter heartens.

More stories.

More "remember whens."

What could be richer?

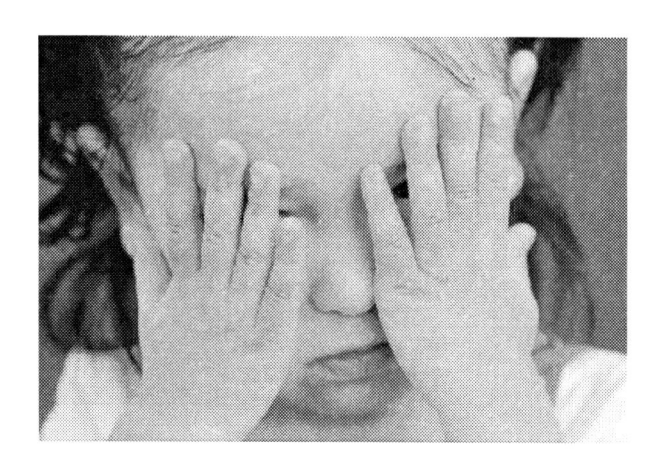

Hmm...

# I Feel Like a Child

*Been away for so long and have so many things to tell you.*

*Feel like a child.*

*Show and tell in school.*

*Music.*

*Dance.*

*Poems.*

*Moments.*

*Thoughts.*

*Always want to be a Child.*

*Things are fun.*

*Things are positive and amazing.*

*And now...
Little things are so noticeable.*

*Sure hope I can share them with a best friend.*

Hmm...

# Friend

Spoke to a special friend.

She always asks first -
how are you?

So engaged...
Had to stop
and ask her
how are you?

She told me she fell.

A compressed fracture.

It's a long story and
I feel responsible.

My best friend.

Here I am in the sun.

She is in a hospital bed
asking about me.

That is how she is.

Everyone else comes first.

Hmm...

# Hope

It is so easy to be self absorbed.

Not noticing
hurtful things.

We are people of hope.

It will be okay.

We bury our fears.

When they surface
we are vulnerable.

Perhaps that is good.

At least we know
we're human.

And there is hope
that things can be better.

Hmm...

## Decisions

*Big decisions.*

*Big day.*

*Big decisions.*

*Some irreversible.*

*Fear.*

*Placing faith in someone hardly known.*

*Trust.*

*Education.*

*Judgment.*

*Instincts.*

*Expect much.*

*Hopefully, disappointment will not follow.*

Hmm...

## The Day

*Beautiful day.*

*Friends.*

*Activities.*

*Taken for granted.*

*Life is simple.*

*The world makes it complicated.*

*Demands so much.*

*We must live.*

*Appreciate.*

*Notice.*

*And just be.*

Hmm...

## It Is So Hard

It is so hard
to just be a little girl.

Always under someone's wing.

Never stunning.
Gorgeous.
Commanding.
Sophisticated.

You reached out.

Seemingly attracted
to something.

Heaven knows what.

It will never be.

Not in the cards.

But know that I could love you
for the things you
don't know that you give to me.

Hmm...

## Remember

I sit in all this opulence.

Seems complicated.

Could I live with this?
I doubt it.

It does remind me.

Life can be simple
and still be fulfilling.

Hmm...

## Mending

*An aching soul.*

*Impossible to mend.*

*Impossible to touch.*

*How is it possible
to feel something
intangible?*

*Impossible
to mend.*

*But enriches the soul.*

Hmm...

## What Does it Mean?

*She was just a little girl
or so she thought.*

*Pixie cut.*

*Fair skin.*

*Simple, pretty smile.*

*Very nice clothes.*

*And a car
she could hardly afford.*

*What did it all mean
to her?*

*Why did she have it?*

*Used to it?*

*Made her feel grown up?*

*Or just a substitute
for something greater?*

Hmm...

Westport, New York
2004

## Lassie

*By my side.*

*Always protecting.*

*Calm and comfortable.*

*Can't imagine being without her.*

*Just a part of my life.*

*My other soul.*

Hmm...

## Children

*A wonderful gift
for a woman to give.*

*Special feelings
to receive from one
starting out so young.*

*Each is unique.*

*Wanting to be noticed.*

*Not for the obvious.*

Hmm...

# Mellow

The sounds of the water.

It mesmerizes me
and my thoughts.

I want to move
forever with the
natural flow.

And forget about the
world I currently know.

The stress has been
great.

Not always worth the price.

The water beckons.

May it always be
some place I can go to for peace.

Hmm...

## From Nowhere

A friend.

Out of nowhere.

All of a sudden
a special friend.

Our paths do not cross
every day,
but our thoughts do.

Beginning to learn
what is really important.

It is not goals.

Objectives.

Money
or glory.

It's my friend.

Hmm...

# Clouds

Cumulus clouds
hang over the ocean.

Protect beachgoers from the sun.

The tide reminds observers
that the ocean is king.

The morning
before the crowd
is best.

Feet in the sand.

Enjoying the serenity
and the solitude.

Notice the clouds.

Hmm...

# Footprints

Footprints in the sand.

Men.

Women.

Children.

Meshed together.

Some disappear into the ocean.

All have a destination
coming to an invisible end.

Hmm...

# Rhythm

Soon to return
to life's normal rhythm.

Serving others.

Following rules.

Will my mind adjust?

Will my heart respond?

Life is so precious.

Priorities are a wonderful thing.

Remember them.

It will make the rhythm possible.

Hmm...

# She

*A surprise.*

*A gift.*

*So simple.*

*From the heart.*

*Brings a smile.*

*Amazing
how easy she is to please.*

Hmm...

## Gifts

They can be lavish.

Expensive.

Noticeable.

Show-stoppers.

Debt producing.

Thoughtful.

Unexpected.

Fun.

Appreciated.

Or just loved.

Hmm...

## Explore

Love your life.

Time to explore
who you are.

Opportunities create
a language we must understand.

The moments
are all yours.

Seize them
without regret.

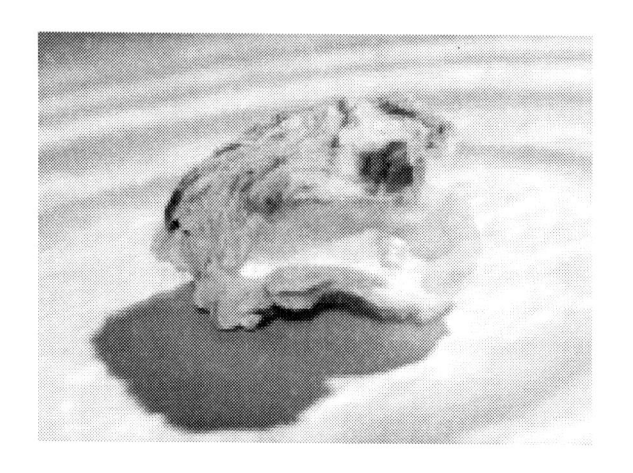

Hmm...

## Perfect

Will I ever find a pearl?

The perfect gem
along a shore.

A fantasy.

My own discovery.

Not acquired in a an easy way
but through
my own dreams.

Yes, the pearl.

It only takes one oyster.

Where are you?

Answer me.

I will care for you.

Hmm...

## On A Winter Night

On a winter night
I thought of you.

My old and
loyal friend.

We used to meet for lunch.

Play all kinds of games.

Return to our lives
on a winter night.

Once we even had dinner.

We parted again.

On a winter night.

Hmm...

## It's Never Enough

A tear fell
while looking at the mist.

It's not sadness.

It's the beauty of life.

It's never enough
for the soul.

Hmm...

## And So

*And so
there were changes to be made.*

*And so
it was not comfortable for some.*

*And so
we made them slowly.*

*And so
the smiles became fewer.*

*And so
we wondered.*

Hmm...

# Once

Once
I had
a perfect feeling.

It was just a moment.

A short span of time.

That's okay.

For it was special
in my mind.

Just one moment
to be captured.

Hmm...

## The Third Dimension

A peace
discovered by the soul
at its core.

When you find it,
treasure the moment.

Extend your hand
to the spirit.

For that's all it is.

Never to be embraced.

Only to be adored.

Hmm...

## Notre Dame

The Golden Dome.

The Fight Song.

The Cathedral.

Some love it.

Some hate it.

No one can deny its spirit.

Hmm...

# The Kiss

A touching connection...

Hmm...

## The Greatest Gift

The greatest gift
when two souls embrace.

Inner peace.

!

Epilogue...just for you

Hmm...

Imagine

!